Hi! My name is Mike. I'm an author, travel nurse, set medic, musician, and avid snowboarder from Tennessee. I hope you enjoy reading this story as much as I enjoyed writing it!

In the lively city of Nashville, there lived a little boy by the name of Prince. Prince loved to play basketball and football games, usually under the Friday night lights, to fully enjoy the weekends.

Whenever he played his favourite games, his dreadlocks flew behind him, and he was good at whatever he played.

"One day, his dad, Chris, told him, "Prince, we're moving to another place," his own dreadlocks resembled his son's. "Which place, Dad?" Prince replied. "Dillon, Colorado.

It's a ski town," Chris answered, expecting Prince to digest the news. "But Dad, I don't know anything about snowboarding," Prince said in a worried manner.

Their Father-Son conversation didn't last long as Chris had to leave for work. Finally, the family moved to Dillon. Dillon was very different from Nashville.

The snow-capped mountains were beautiful, but to Prince, they were alien and scary.

On his first day at the new school, Prince tried to make friends and fit in, but it did not work. "Any of you play basketball?" Prince asked hopefully. "Here?" a boy with blonde hair laughed. "Playing basketball in the snow is like finding a swimming pool in a desert."

The day ended back home. Prince complained to his father, "I don't fit in here, Dad. Everybody laughs at me and makes fun of my hair. Nobody plays basketball here."

Chris sat down next to him. He talked in a gentle tone, "Keep trying, son. What if you played the same sports they enjoy and discover another kind of freedom?"

Prince, being a good son, agreed with his father and the next day, with complete dedication, he rented a snowboard and headed for the mountain. He looked around and found kids gliding easily on the snow, feeling stuck and like an outsider. He asked Chris, "Dad, what if I can't do this?" Chris put his hand on Prince's shoulder, looking into his eyes. "Son, practice makes perfect. Remember your first basketball game? You couldn't even bounce the ball."

Prince took a deep breath and got on his snowboard. He slid like an amoeba on his first try, moving all jiggly wiggly on the snow before falling on his face. However, each time he fell, he got right back up, as if he was enjoying it on the inside.

He kept trying since it was about proving to the world and to himself that he could do new things and not just do them but also be good at them.

"Hey, for a first-timer, you are doing a great job!" someone shouted out loud. Prince searched around and saw a girl about his age, smiling and excited. It was Sydney, a future friend from school.

Despite the first time on the slopes being a complete disaster, Prince and a few other first-timers formed a group and laughed at themselves and each other.

Prince made friends with Felix, who hated the cold as much as cats hate water, and Bradley, who was good at physics but couldn't understand the physics of snowboarding one bit.

Sydney was the only one in the group who could actually ride with ease. "Gravity just loves Prince, doesn't it?" Bradley joked as Prince face-planted in the snow once again.

As time went by, all the hours and fun put in by Prince began to show results. He started to shine in snowboarding as well, turning heads and proving those people wrong who thought Prince could only be good at basketball.

Sydney motivated the group to take part in the Dillon Derby next week. "We should all enter. Show what we got!" She said excitedly. Prince hesitated. "I am not sure if I am ready to compete." "It's not about winning, Prince, it's about having fun as a group," Felix said.

When the day of the competition arrived, the jury, sitting on their benches, were shocked to see a young black kid with dreadlocks entering the ski area, with his snowboard tucked underneath his arm.

Only after a while, Prince's run, filled with creativity born from his background in other sports, made his final jump. A bold move that combined a basketball dunk motion with a snowboard grab made the audience gasp.

As he went past the finish line, everyone cheered from the stands. "You've got some serious moves; you are a star, kid," an experienced snowboarder told him afterwards. Never seen anything quite like it.

Finally, Prince had found his rhythm in Dillon within the community. Just as his interest grew in snowboarding, the community was taking an interest in basketball.

After the cheerful episode, Chris and Prince were sitting on their porch looking out over the mountains. "You know, I never thought I wouldn't fit in here, Dad, but I found something that I didn't even know I was looking for," Prince said. Chris nodded in agreement with pride in his chest and eyes. "You've grown so much. Not just as a snowboarder, but as a person. Dillon's lucky to have you!"

Prince had found that being different wasn't a barrier, but an opportunity to win over a new challenge and grow. And in this new chapter, he wasn't just a visitor. He was home.